Simone,

T0049221

half & half

CHRISTINE RODRIGUEZ

Simone, Half and Half © Copyright 2022 by Christine Rodriguez

For professional or amateur production rights, please contact Playwrights Canada Press

LIBRARY AND ARCHIVES CANADA CATALOGUING IN PUBLICATION
Title: Simone, half and half / Christine Rodriguez.
Names: Rodriguez, Christine (Author of Simone, half and half), author.
Description: A play
Identifiers: Canadiana (print) 20220257744 | Canadiana (ebook) 20220258317
  | ISBN 9780369103765 (softcover) | ISBN 9780369103789 (PDF)
  | ISBN 9780369103772 (HTML)
Classification: LCC PS8635.03737 S56 2022 | DDC C812/.6—dc23

Playwrights Canada Press operates on land which is the ancestral home of the Anishinaabe Nations (Ojibwe / Chippewa, Odawa, Potawatomi, Algonquin, Saulteaux, Nipissing, and Mississauga), the Wendat, and the members of the Haudenosaunee Confederacy (Mohawk, Oneida, Onondaga, Cayuga, Seneca, and Tuscarora), as well as Metis and Inuit peoples. It always was and always will be Indigenous land.

We acknowledge the support of the Canada Council for the Arts, the Ontario Arts Council (OAC), Ontario Creates, and the Government of Canada for our publishing activities.

For Mom and Dad

Foreword

By Quincy Armorer

I have long been obsessed with the spectrum of mixed-race heritage and how the many labels and categories used to define me never felt fully accurate or complete. I thought often about my ancestors, many of whom were being omitted or ignored whenever one aspect of my identity was prioritized or favoured over all the others. This obsession led to an overwhelming desire to create a piece of theatre that centred on the experience of a young, mixed-race person struggling with where and with whom they belong.

Christine Rodriguez and I worked together for several years at Black Theatre Workshop. I was the artistic director and Christine was the coordinator of our annual Black History Month School Tour. We often found ourselves alone together in the office, and there were many lengthy one-on-one conversations about anything and everything—our lives, our families, our dreams, but mostly about our art. I always appreciated these talks with Christine; her strong-willed, bold, firm, unapologetic, steadfast thoughts and opinions were always matched with an openness and generosity of spirit that allowed for her to listen and, especially, hear. I admire this quality in her greatly. It was during one of these many conversations when it became very clear to me that the embryo of that play growing in my brain was asking for Christine to be its surrogate.

Christine brought so much more to *Simone, Half and Half* than I could have anticipated. Her writing is full of passion and heart and drive and commitment, and these qualities are infused in all the characters. She brought our shared Trinidad and Tobago heritage, celebrating its music and history and culture. She brought her love of art and her devotion to activism as central elements to the storytelling. Most especially, she brought humour and hope and joy. What we are left with is a portrait of a young person who is struggling with, accepting, and ultimately celebrating all that makes her who she is—fully, completely, without excuse or apology.

There were several new plays commissioned during my time as artistic director at Black Theatre Workshop, but *Simone, Half and Half* differs from the others. This play was always intended to be a journey of the mind, a journey of the self, and a journey of the soul. It's about understanding where we find our self-worth and how much value we place on the thoughts and opinions of others. There is often a very real "othering" of multiracial people as well as a pressure to choose a single box to put ourselves into. This discrimination can exist not only toward the Black communities but also within them. Simone's journey is navigating all the negative forces she feels and finding peace, hope, and especially joy in simply being who she is.

During the original production, a large part of the experience for me was watching our young audiences and noticing when and how they found themselves reflected in the play. It was clear to me that many of them felt as though they were seeing their own story for the very first time. I always loved hearing their feedback, but I especially loved the silent responses—the quiet focus of being fully engaged, forward, present, taking the story in, and clearly feeling it resonate within. In many ways, *Simone, Half and Half* felt long overdue, that an audience had been eager for its characters—its humour, heart, and joy—for quite some time, and were merely waiting for Christine to bring it to life.

Quincy Armorer has worked professionally as an actor, director, instructor, and administrator for over twenty years. As an actor, he has worked at the Stratford Festival, National Arts Centre, Centaur Theatre, Black Theatre Workshop, St. Lawrence Shakespeare Festival, Geordie Theatre, Repercussion Theatre, Imago Theatre, Piggery Theatre, and Shakespeare by the Sea, among many others. An alumnus of both the Theatre Department at Concordia University and the Birmingham Conservatory for Classical Theatre at the Stratford Festival, Quincy is Adjunct Professor at Queen's University, Associate Director of the Acting Program (English Section) at the National Theatre School of Canada, and was Artistic Director of Black Theatre Workshop from 2011 to 2021.

Production History

Simone, Half and Half was commissioned by Black Theatre Workshop through a grant from the Cole Foundation's Intercultural Conversations program. The play received dramaturgical support from Dean Fleming and Emma Tibaldo through Playwrights' Workshop Montréal. The play also received funding for writing workshops through the Canada Council for the Arts with actors Daniela Sandiford, Alexandra Laferrière, Jen Viens, Anton Sebastian May, Dakota Jamal Wellman, Eleanor Noble, Jahlani Knorren, Briauna James, Keren Roberts, Daryn Jack, Katherine Sideris, Bridgett Williams, and Samantha Pioretti; directors Dayane Ntibarikure and Quincy Armorer; set and costume designer Nalo Soyini Bruce; and continued dramaturgical support from Dean Fleming and Marie Barlizo. A special thanks to Akido Trim, of Trinidad and Tobago, for some of the cultural specificities.

The play was first produced by Black Theatre Workshop in February 2020 for a Black History Month school tour, visiting schools across the greater Montreal region, and for two public performances in Montreal at Union United Church and at the Black Community Resource Centre, with the following cast and creative team:

Vanessa: Alexandra Laferrière
Sarah: Jennifer Roberts
Simone: Autumn Taylor
Jay: Dakota Jamal Wellman

Director: Quincy Armorer
Consulting Director: Amanda Kellock
Technical Director: Tristynn Duheme
Video Projection Design: HAUI, a.k.a. Howard Davis
Set and Costume Design: Nalo Soyini Bruce
Assistant Set and Costume Design: Holly Hilts and Courtney
Moses Orbin
Sound Design: Rob Denton
Choreography: Patrick Park
Stage Manager: Sandi Becker

Characters

SIMONE: A fourteen-year-old girl who has a White mother and Black father. She is in grade eight.

SARAH: A fourteen-year-old girl who is White. Simone's best friend since kindergarten.

JAY: A fourteen-year-old boy who is Black. A friend Simone made in grade seven.

VANESSA: A sixteen-year-old girl who is Black and in grade ten. Leader of the Black History and Culture Committee (BHCC).

PRINCIPAL, MOM, AND VOICES: Other characters that appear only in voice-over.

Scene

The play takes place in a suburban Montreal high school (grades seven to eleven), where students of colour are a minority.

Time

The present.

Scene 1

SIMONE's bedroom.

SIMONE writes in her journal as voices in her head are heard aloud.

ADULT AND CHILDREN'S VOICES: Half-and-half. Half-breed. Half-caste. Half-blood. Coloured. Quadroon. Octoroon. Mixed-race. Mixed-up. Messed-up. Mulatto.

SIMONE: *(as she writes the word down in her journal)* M-i-s-c-e-g-e-n-a-t-i-o-n.

SIMONE's train of thought continues as she addresses the audience.

Miscegenation. Sounds like a science experiment . . . These are the words that have been used to describe people like me. But what's in a word or in these words or any words? What are the words that really say who I am? I am. I am. Here I am . . . Why do you need the words? What if there isn't one word? My mom can trace her family back to the 1600s to this one spot in the north of France. A name and a place. Daniel Parent, Tourcoing, Nord-Pas-de-Calais. But my dad can't do that. He can only go as far back as Trinidad and Tobago. A dark-skinned woman. Soledad Rouseau. My great-

great-grandmother. An old woman who spoke little as she sat in her rocking chair watching the world change before her eyes. That's all my grandmother remembers. Was she a slave when she was a child? Or were her parents slaves? What did she see? What did she know? It's all gone now. We'll never know where she came from or what she believed or what cultural practices she had that came from her faraway homeland. Just an old Black woman on a Caribbean island. To know and not to know.

"Where are you from?" Everywhere. "What are you?" I don't know.

Change of lighting.

Scene 2

A hip hop song blares. SIMONE jumps into practising a dance routine with her best friend, SARAH. SIMONE makes a misstep.

SIMONE: Oops.

SARAH: Oh my God! Get it right! Come on! Let's start over.

SIMONE: Okay . . .

SARAH and SIMONE repeat the dance moves. They're good; they've taken many lessons. They know what they're doing . . . except . . . SIMONE makes a wrong step again.

I'm sorry.

SARAH: You're getting on my nerves.

SIMONE: I'm—

SARAH: Sorry. I know. I swear, it's like you're not even Black! Let's start over.

SIMONE: I'm sorry but I have to—

SARAH: No!

SIMONE: Yes! We're going to the jump up, remember?

SARAH: No, I don't.

SIMONE: You're coming, right?

SARAH: No.

SIMONE: Why not?

SARAH: I don't feel like it.

SIMONE: It'll be fun.

SARAH: It won't be.

SIMONE: Of course it'll be. There'll be music—

SARAH: I hate that loud music.

SIMONE: And dancing—

SARAH: I really don't feel comfortable going.

SIMONE: What do you mean?

SARAH: Everybody . . . I'll be the only White person there.

SIMONE: You won't be. Anyway . . . you're going there to hang out with me, right?

SARAH: Uh, you're going to hang out with Jay.

SIMONE: Please come. It's our last chance to hang out before I go away to summer camp . . .

Beat.

JAY enters.

JAY: Yo!

SARAH: Oh, hey! Hi!

SIMONE: Hi . . .

SIMONE quickly gathers her things to leave.

JAY: How's the routine going?

SARAH: Fantastic!

JAY: You guys are really good.

SARAH: Aww, thanks!

SIMONE: *(ready to leave)* You're sure you won't come?

SARAH: Yes. I'm sure.

SIMONE: *(to JAY)* Fine . . . let's go.

JAY: Uh, okay. Bye.

SARAH: Bye!!

> *SIMONE doesn't look back. JAY follows SIMONE out. They head for a bus stop.*

JAY: Why isn't she coming?

SIMONE: She—she has a headache.

JAY: Are you okay?

SIMONE: Yes . . . yes. I'm excited about the jump up.

JAY: Jump up.

SIMONE: Yah?

JAY: We don't say "the" jump up.

> *Beat.*

Whatever. You're gonna love it! We're gonna zess!

SIMONE: Zess??

JAY: More zessin', less stressin'. You know? Have fun. You have to let go. Set yo'self free!

SIMONE: Haha, okay . . . ?

JAY: How can I put it . . .

> *Beat.*

It's like those people who crawl up the steps to the oratory on their knees. It's hard. It's hot. The sun beats down on you, but, man, when you're done, you feel like a new person. It's like a rite . . . huh . . . a rite of . . .

SIMONE: A rite of passage.

JAY: Exactly! And it helps me stay connected to my Trini roots.

SIMONE: How?

JAY: *(laughs)* Girl, don't you know anything about where you come from?

> *SIMONE pouts.*

Jump up started hundreds of years ago in Trinidad. We're celebrating freedom from slavery. Freedom to do whatever we damn well please.

SIMONE: I didn't know that . . .

JAY: Are you sure you're all right?

SIMONE: I'm fine. Here comes the bus!

Change of lighting.

Scene 3

Carifiesta. Soca music plays. SIMONE and JAY dance calmly. Step, step, step, step.

Jumping. Just like JAY said, they start to feel the bacchanal. They start to really let loose. Like a sort of dream.

Things wash away . . . They let it all out . . .

JAY and SIMONE rest in a park downtown once jump up is over.

SIMONE: You were right.

JAY: About?

SIMONE: Feeling like a new person.

JAY: Ya see?!

SIMONE: I never jumped up before.

JAY: Never?

SIMONE: My dad's not into stuff like this . . .

JAY: Next time we should play mas.

SIMONE: What's that?

JAY: Masquerade. Join a band and wear a costume.

SIMONE: We can do that?

JAY: Yah. Anyone can do it. You just have to pay and they give you a costume.

SIMONE: Oh cool! Does it come from Africa?

JAY: Not exactly. It comes from the French who used to do masquerades.

SIMONE: The French? I thought Trinidad was a British colony.

JAY: It was. But first it was Spanish. Then came French people and their slaves who all spoke French. I think . . . from Martinique and Guadeloupe. Maybe Saint-Domingue?

SIMONE: *(in Québécois French)* Ah ben.

JAY: Ah ben. You know, I have a book you need to read. I found it in my dad's library. It's got a lot of great info.

SIMONE: What would I do without you!

JAY: You'd be stuck with Sarah.

SIMONE: *(laughing)* Oh my God!!!!!

JAY: I got you to smile!

SIMONE: *(tries not to laugh)* No, you didn't!

JAY: Yah, yah, you see, right there! That's a smile.

> *Suddenly there's the bleep of a police siren. JAY's mood instantly changes.*

Humph. We have to go.

SIMONE: Why?

JAY: It's just that time.

> *SIMONE looks around.*

SIMONE: Why are the police making everyone leave the park?

JAY: Cuz that's how they do.

SIMONE: But we're not doing anything.

JAY: It doesn't matter.

> *SIMONE has to rush to catch up to JAY. A fun day comes to an abrupt end.*
>
> *Change of lighting.*

Scene 4

SIMONE has her bags ready to go off to summer camp. She hears voices again.

ADULT AND CHILDREN'S VOICES: You have a big nose. You're pretty for a Black person. You have good hair. Happy Nappy. Not too kinky. If we stick a pick in your hair, will it stay in or will it fall out?

SIMONE: *(to audience)* Every summer, my mom sends me to camp. She loved it so much as a kid. I guess she thinks that I will too. But when I get there, there's no one there like me. Who looks like me. Who has hair like me. My mom warns me every time to keep my hair braided or in ponytails because no one at the camp will know what to do. You know what? She's right. Once I came back from camp with a big wad of hair in the back of my head in a tangle of knots, one big bird nest in the back—right here. I'm not kidding. But aside from the hair problem, camp's not too bad . . . Everyone is pretty nice. It's not their fault they don't know what to do with my hair. But it feels strange to always stand out as the lone Blackish person. So, I kind of don't say much. That way I don't stand out too much. And I pray I'll make that one good friend that I can click with, and we'll spend the whole camp time together like BFFs. It's always someone a little different, a bit of a geek, like me. But it always works. It ends up being fun that way. But if I don't end up meeting that one right person, it ends up being long and lonely.

SIMONE leaves for camp.

Scene 5

SIMONE and SARAH run into each other on the first day back to school and hug.

SARAH: Oh my God! I'm so glad school's starting again!

SIMONE: I know, right?

SARAH: I bet you can't wait to see Jay!

SIMONE: What?

SARAH: Oh, don't what me. You always do that to cover up what you really think.

SIMONE: I do not.

SARAH: Yes, you do. You've been doing it since kindergarten!

SIMONE: I have not.

SARAH: Yes, you have!

SIMONE: Have. Not.

SARAH: You bore me so much.

SIMONE: Ha! Not half as much as you bore me!

They laugh as they walk by a school poster.

SARAH: Oh look! The auditions for the talent show are in November!

SIMONE: Cool.

SARAH: You're ready for this, right?

SIMONE: I am.

SARAH: You have to be. Like, we need to be in the show. We need to be stars.

SIMONE: Yah, I guess . . .

SARAH: Don't guess.

SIMONE: I mean . . . I'm gonna try to do my best . . .

SARAH: Simone, I'm counting on you. It's you and me. I can't do this without you. You know that, right? Like, there's no way a solo piece is gonna be as good as a duo.

SIMONE: Okay.

SARAH: I've been dreaming of this since I was little! All those shows we put on in our basements.

SIMONE: Mm-hmm.

SARAH: Think about it! It's gonna be a real show with a real audience. Oh my God! We have to do well. More than that. We have to be great! But most of all, we can't embarrass ourselves in front of the whole school.

SIMONE: *(looking at the poster more closely)* Oh look! It's for charity.

SARAH: It is?

SIMONE: Yah, it says right here. For an orphanage in Malawi.

SARAH: Even more reason to kick butt. For the African kids!

SIMONE: For the Malawian kids.

SARAH: Right. Malawi. Africa. You know what I mean.

JAY appears.

SIMONE: Hey!

JAY: Hey!

SARAH: Why hello!

JAY: *(self-consciously)* Uh, hello.

JAY pulls something out of his backpack and hands it to SIMONE.

Here's the book I promised you.

SIMONE: Oh, wow! This is so great!

SIMONE takes hold of the book and holds it with reverence as she flips through the yellowed pages.

SARAH: What's that?

SARAH grabs the book to read the title.

The history of Trinidad and Tobago???

SIMONE takes the book from SARAH's hands.

SIMONE: *(to JAY)* Thank you so much.

SARAH: We went to Jamaica once for a vacation. It was lit.

JAY and SIMONE exchange glances.

He pulls out his cellphone.

JAY: Check this out.

He shows SIMONE an email on his phone. SARAH tries to see but can't.

This girl I know, Vanessa, she's so in tune. She's getting a group of us together to push for more Black history and culture in our classes.

SIMONE: Really?

SARAH laughs.

JAY and SIMONE look at her.

SARAH: You already have a month!

JAY: Yah . . . right . . .

(to SIMONE*)* First meeting is today after school. Imma be there.

The bell rings.

Catch you later.

SIMONE: Later.

SARAH, amused, watches SIMONE*.*

What?

SARAH: Whatevs. So, my house after school.

SIMONE: I'm not sure . . .

SARAH: We have to come up with costumes for the auditions.

SIMONE: Yaaah . . .

SARAH: Yaaah?

SIMONE: I'm thinking of checking that group out.

SIMONE: You can't be serious.

SIMONE: I am.

SARAH: The school's not going to change what they teach, especially not for a small group of students.

SIMONE: You don't know that—

SARAH: Simone! You don't have time for this anyway. We have the audition to get ready for.

SIMONE: I think I have time . . .

SARAH: No, you don't.

SIMONE: I do.

> *Beat.*

SARAH: Okay, fine. We'll go to the meeting. We can work on costumes tomorrow.

SIMONE: I don't . . .

SARAH: You don't what?

SIMONE: I don't think it's for . . . The email said they only want Black students to join the group . . .

SARAH: Isn't that kind of racist?

SIMONE: I . . . don't know . . . maybe . . . ?

SARAH: But you're only half-Black . . .

SIMONE: I really want to check this group out. Find out more about what they want to do.

SARAH: You mean find out more about Jay!!

SIMONE: It's not about Jay.

SARAH: *(laughing at SIMONE)* A little bit, though . . .

SIMONE: *(laughs)* Well . . . it doesn't matter what you think. I'm going to the meeting and . . . that's that.

SARAH: Okay. Fine. But costume design is tomorrow then.

SIMONE: Tomorrow.

SARAH: Tomorrow!

The school bell rings. They run to class.

Scene 6

After school, JAY and VANESSA sit in a classroom, waiting to start the inaugural Black History and Culture Committee meeting.

VANESSA: I thought we'd get a bigger turnout . . .

JAY: We should wait a few more minutes . . .

VANESSA: They're like sheep! They're all being brainwashed by social media and basketball. They don't even know what they don't know.

JAY shrugs and pulls out a Black Panther comic book to read while he's waiting.

That's what you're feeding your mind with?

JAY flashes her a Wakanda forever sign.

VANESSA shakes her head.

SIMONE appears timidly in the doorway.

JAY: *(Trini accent)* Hey! Simone! Wah' goin' on?

VANESSA: *(to SIMONE)* What are you doing here?

JAY: Vanessa, this is my friend, Simone.

VANESSA: I know who she is, but why is she here?

SIMONE: Huh . . . I . . . hmm . . .

VANESSA: I need people who can speak in this group.

SIMONE: I can speak . . . I can speak.

VANESSA: And what do you know about Black history and culture?

SIMONE: I . . . know about Dr. Martin Luther King Jr. and Malcom X . . .

VANESSA stares blankly at SIMONE.

I'm gonna read this book Jay lent me!

SIMONE pulls the book out of her backpack and reads the title.

History of the People of Trinidad and Tobago. By Dr. Eric Williams.

VANESSA: The first prime minister of Trinidad and Tobago, after it gained independence.

SIMONE: He was?

VANESSA: *(to JAY)* This is what I have to work with?!

SIMONE: I'm sorry. I can do more reading and research. I promise.

VANESSA gives JAY side-eye.

JAY: *(to VANESSA)* Beggars can't be choosers.

VANESSA: All right. Grab a seat. I can see I have my work cut out with the both of you.

VANESSA stands more formally. She clears her throat and begins her prepared speech. JAY and SIMONE sit, ready to take notes as they listen.

We are meeting here today to take charge of telling our own history. Choose what's important to us. Educate people about stories they don't know but that are important contributions to the modern world and especially to Canada.

JAY and SIMONE smile at each other and flirt. VANESSA doesn't notice right away. But then gives them the evil eye.

We're sick and tired of being treated like we aren't important. Like we haven't done anything to build this continent. We're going to show them that we belong here as much as the next person. This is Black people taking control of our destiny.

JAY: *(taking notes)* Destiny . . .

VANESSA: Because if you don't know where you come from, you sure as hell don't know where you're going.

(to SIMONE and JAY) Hey! Are you here to fool around or to change the world?

(to SIMONE directly) This is not some get-to-explore-your-Blackness group. We have work to do!

SIMONE: Yes, yes, right!

VANESSA: *(to JAY and SIMONE)* Do you know any Black poets?

SIMONE and JAY answer at the same time.

JAY: Yes!

SIMONE: No . . .

VANESSA: Do you know any Black playwrights?

SIMONE and JAY answer at the same time.

JAY: Yes!

SIMONE: No . . .

VANESSA: Do you know any Black visual artists?

SIMONE and JAY answer at the same time.

JAY: Yes!

SIMONE: No . . .

VANESSA: *(to JAY, pointing at SIMONE)* That there is exactly the problem we need to fix.

Change of lighting.

Scene 7

JAY and SIMONE walk home from school.

JAY: Boiii, we are gonna have to do so much work to get this group going. I thought for sure more people would show up. Dang. Where're all the socially aware people at?

Beat.

You're really quiet.

SIMONE: I don't know about this group . . .

JAY: What do you mean?

SIMONE: I don't think that Vanessa likes me very much.

JAY: Vanessa? She's like that with everyone. She sets the bar high.

SIMONE: Maybe that's why no one wants to join.

JAY: Probably.

SIMONE: I don't know how I can help.

JAY: You have to stay . . . We need you. We have nobody else.

SIMONE: Thanks!

JAY: No! I mean, lots of people don't know anything. I just read that one book about Trinidad.

SIMONE: That's it?!

JAY: Well . . . You have to start somewhere. So I'm gonna listen and learn. If we can put something good together, we can change the school and everyone can start to learn something.

SIMONE: Is it really okay for me to be in this committee if I'm not really Black?

JAY: Simone, you have brown skin. Every day of your life is about being Black. You're not a chameleon.

SIMONE: No but—

JAY: You don't need to ask whether you belong or are good enough. We need your help—besides, I'm gonna die if you leave me alone with Vanessa. Puhleazzz.

SIMONE: She's kinda bossy.

JAY: She's fierce, but don't let her push you around. You're super smart.

SIMONE: I am?

JAY: Yah!

SIMONE: Haha. So are you!

Change of lighting.

Scene 8

JAY helps VANESSA carry boxes filled with material into a classroom ahead of the next Black History and Culture Committee meeting, which is set to begin in a few minutes.

VANESSA: I think we should look at one topic or theme each year that students can learn about, to keep it simple. You know, like, Angélique. You read books about her, read the play, do research on the topic or things related to it. Like we could even do a mock trial or something. Then the next year . . .

VANESSA notices SIMONE arrive.

Oh Lawd! Here comes the White soul woman.

JAY can't help but chuckle. SIMONE is on a mission though.

SIMONE: I found so much great stuff after the meeting when I got home. Did you know that Dorothy Dandridge was the first Black woman nominated in the best actress category for an Oscar in 1954.

Only ten Black women have been nominated for lead actress in the

Oscars's ninety-one year history, and only one Black woman has actually received the Oscar: Halle Berry in 2001. Ninety-one years of Oscars and only one Black woman has received the Oscar for lead actress.

Except, Halle Berry's mother is white. Which I find interesting because it means that people who are mixed race are also important contributors to Black arts and culture and political movements.

Blackness is in fact a rainbow of colours. Look at Angela Davis, a warrior for civil rights in the 1960s. She's a very light shade of Black. Yet that does not stop her from fighting for civil rights for ALL Black people. And Viola Desmond is Canada's very own civil rights hero.

VANESSA: Okay, great. So you did some research.

SIMONE: *(before VANESSA can walk away)* Viola Desmond was mixed race. She had a white mother and a Black father, just like me.

VANESSA stares at SIMONE, assessing her.

VANESSA: You're nothing like Viola Desmond though. She was a member of the Black community. She made and sold beauty products for Black women. What have you ever done for Black women, Simone?

SIMONE: I spent a lot of time on this . . .

VANESSA: And what? You think you deserve a medal because you did one day's worth of work?

SIMONE: I, uh, no . . . I just meant to point out that I can help even though . . .

SIMONE's voice trails off as she watches VANESSA lift a pile of boxes from behind the desk full of printouts, articles, and books.

VANESSA: I've been pulling together all this stuff for months now. We're gonna go through all of it and find the things that are the most important to start with—the things that never get talked about but should be.

VANESSA gives a box to JAY.

(passionately sifting through her files) Here's stuff about enslaved African Americans who were freed and came to settle in Ontario after the War of 1812. Oh, and this is about Angélique, who was accused of burning down Montreal in 1734. And this is about the first race riot in North America that happened in Nova Scotia.

JAY: *(sifting through the files)* Wow . . .

VANESSA gives another box to SIMONE. VANESSA pulls out a particular folder.

VANESSA: Here! You oughta like this one. It's about this guy James Douglas who helped establish British Colombia. He's mixed race like you. He was half Scottish, half Antiguan, born in Guyana. But Indigenous people hated him because he worked for the Hudson's Bay Company.

SIMONE: *(taking the files from VANESSA)* You've done a lot of work.

VANESSA: Yes. I have.

Silence falls over them as they dig into the boxes. The group is forming as they start to collectively work together.

Change of lighting.

Scene 9

Commercial hip hop music plays again. SARAH and SIMONE practise their dance moves. SIMONE makes a mistake.

SARAH: Not again! Can you get with the program!

SIMONE snarls in discouragement. She walks over to get a drink from her water bottle and sits down. She wipes the sweat off her face and neck with a towel.

What's the matter now?

SIMONE: I need a break.

SARAH: I told you this was all gonna be too much.

SIMONE: It's not. I just need a break.

SARAH: You have too much on your plate.

SIMONE: No. It's just . . . I'm having trouble sleeping.

SARAH: Because you're stressed.

SIMONE: I have these nightmares where I hear voices and get called names and—

SARAH: That sounds crazy.

SIMONE: Names like mulatto.

SARAH: You are mulatto.

SIMONE: It means "little mule" in Spanish.

SARAH shrugs.

A mule is half a stallion, half a donkey. Which part of me do you think is the stallion and which is the donkey?

SARAH is uncharacteristically speechless.

You know, your dad once called me that.

SARAH: *(genuinely surprised)* What?!

SIMONE: We were about eight years old. I was at your house, and we were playing with Barbies in the living room while your dad was reading a book. I think you went to the bathroom. And while you were gone, he leaned toward me and said, "Do you know what you are?" And I said no. And he said to me, "You're mulatto," like it was a bad thing or something. I didn't get it then but . . . It was the way he said it. Mu-lat-tooooo.

SARAH: Why would he do that . . . ?

SIMONE: I don't know . . .

SARAH: But he doesn't speak Spanish . . . I'm sure he has no idea what it means . . . I didn't till you told me just now.

SIMONE: *(introspectively)* Why did he say it that way?

SARAH: I don't know . . .

Beat.

Look, let's forget about all that Black stuff. Let's just dance!!

SIMONE: This music and dancing is Black stuff.

SARAH: Yah, yah. I know! *The Get Down*!
(as an aside) I'm so mad the show was cancelled.
(back on topic) Anyhoo, come on! Let's practise.

SIMONE: I don't feel like it . . .

SARAH: What about the Ma-la-wians?

SIMONE: Don't joke about that.

SARAH: You are so touchy . . . ever since . . .

Beat.

SIMONE: I joined the BHCC?

SARAH: The what?

SIMONE: Black History and Culture Committee. The—

SARAH: BHCC. I get it.

SIMONE: Learning about Black history is allowing me to see why things are the way they are.

SARAH: The past is the past.

SIMONE: That's what a lot of people think. But the past is still affecting us now, like—

> *At this point, VANESSA is walking by the dance studio. She notices SIMONE and SARAH and stays a moment to eavesdrop on their conversation. SIMONE and SARAH are unaware.*

SARAH: Simone! We need to practise.

SIMONE: I'm trying to explain to you—

SARAH: I know. But we really need to rehearse. Come on! Get up!

SIMONE: I don't feel like it.

SARAH: I don't care if you don't feel like it. You promised to do this show with me and you have to see it through. You can't let me down.

> *SIMONE doesn't budge.*

We were friends first, you know. Before Jay came along.

SIMONE: What?!

SARAH: We've been dancing and learning hip hop since grade two!

And all of a sudden you don't feel like dancing anymore? Because of Jay and a committee?

SIMONE: You don't want to understand.

SARAH: I understand this: you are not going to let me down. Do you hear me? It's too late to bail on me. You have to get up and rehearse.

SIMONE remains lethargic.

Simone, my sister from another mother . . .

SIMONE: Mister.

SARAH: Who?

SIMONE: Okay! Let's get back to work.

SARAH: I love you so much! You'll see. This will be awesome. We'll get a standing ovation.

VANESSA leaves.

SIMONE: If you say so . . .

SARAH: No. I swear. We will.

Change of lighting.

Scene 10

Another Black History and Culture Committee meeting.
VANESSA and SIMONE work on their laptops.

VANESSA: All the work you and Jay've done is really good! I mean, I thought I was gonna have to do everything myself. But you did a really good job.

(scrolling through a PowerPoint presentation on the laptop) So year one, the theme will be Angélique, year two Viola Desmond—your favourite—

SIMONE checks her phone for text messages.

Why do you keep checking your phone?

SIMONE: I'm just wondering where Jay's at. It's not like him to miss a meeting.

VANESSA: Lemme ask my brother.

VANESSA texts on her phone and then puts the phone aside.

Are you okay?

SIMONE: I'm supposed to rehearse at five . . . auditions are in two days . . .

VANESSA: So go when you need to.

SIMONE: No. I'm gonna stay till we're done.

VANESSA: You don't have to change your plans on account of—

SIMONE: No, no. This is more important. I mean, if Jay was here to help, but . . .

VANESSA: What about your friend—that White girl—

SIMONE: Sarah.

VANESSA: Yah, isn't she gonna have a meltdown?

SIMONE: I'm more afraid of you.

VANESSA: What?

> *SIMONE smiles.*

Oh my—she made a joke. But seriously, it's your choice. Don't stay if you don't want to—

> *VANESSA's phone pings. She reads the incoming message and puts the phone back down.*

My brother doesn't know where Jay's at.

SIMONE: Oh . . .

VANESSA: You don't have to stay. I'll finish it off on my own.

SIMONE: I'm gonna stay and help.

VANESSA: All right, because it's not something you turn on or off.

SIMONE: Turn what on?

VANESSA: Who you are.

SIMONE: I don't get it.

VANESSA: I know you don't. But I don't have time to preach right now.

SIMONE: No, tell me.

> *Beat.*

VANESSA: I've seen you and Sarah rehearsing. The way she talks to you. We're here working on making ourselves stronger and . . .

SIMONE: And what?

VANESSA: We're always going to come across as angry and bitter, just for speaking up for ourselves, for demanding respect. But we can either try to please people as they step all over us or we can stand up for ourselves and protect ourselves. What is your truth, Simone?

> *SIMONE is silent, trying to find an answer. Her phone pings. She checks quickly.*

Jay?

SIMONE: No, Sarah.

VANESSA: If you're gonna be stressed the whole time, you should just go. It's only gonna stress me out more.

SIMONE: It's just . . . I'm worried about Jay.

VANESSA: Don't worry, dear. He's not cheating on you.

SIMONE: Oh, we're not together.

VANESSA: Mm-hmm.

They turn their focus back to their laptops.

Change of lighting.

Scene 11

Two days later, SIMONE rushes in. SARAH chases after her.

SARAH: Simone. Simone! Don't walk away from me.

SIMONE finally stops and turns to SARAH.

SIMONE: I told you I'm sorry.

SARAH: You were supposed to be ready. One. Hundred. Percent.

SIMONE: All right. I made a small mistake.

SARAH: You should've been ready!

SIMONE: I'm sure the judges didn't notice. You'd have to know the routine.

SARAH: I know the routine. I know what you did.

SIMONE: Don't worry about it. We were good. We'll still make it into the show.

SARAH: That's not the point. We've been planning this for so long—

SIMONE: I have to go.

SARAH: That's exactly what I'm talking about. You put this Black history thing ahead of everything.

SIMONE: Sarah—not today.

Change of lighting.

Scene 12

JAY and SIMONE meet up the next day.

SIMONE carries a portable projector.

SIMONE: Hey, we missed you at the last meeting.

JAY: Sorry . . .

SIMONE: What's going on? You haven't been answering my texts.

JAY: I wasn't feeling well.

SIMONE: Are you feeling better now?

JAY: Yes, I am. Thanks.

SIMONE: I'm glad.

Beat.

VANESSA joins them with her laptop under her arm.

VANESSA: *(to JAY)* Hey! I heard what happened. Are you okay? We can do this without you if you're not feeling up to it.

SIMONE: What happened?

JAY: No. I'm fine.

VANESSA: Okay. Let's do this!

The trio leave to go meet with the principal, all their material and equipment in tow.

Scene 13

Meanwhile, SARAH walks by and checks a list posted on a wall.

She goes down the list and, when she sees her name and SIMONE's, she squeals in delight, hardly able to contain her excitement. She bounces off in search of SIMONE.

Scene 14

Dismayed, the BHCC trio returns, carrying all their stock from their presentation.

SIMONE: It can't be.

VANESSA: "A lot of work and research has gone into creating the current curriculum." They left out almost every aspect of Black history and they think they did a lot of research?

JAY: They only want to listen to the sound of their own voices.

VANESSA: What about all the work and research WE did?! Like, it doesn't count for anything?

JAY: The entire system is made to keep us in our place.

SIMONE: There has to be more to it.

VANESSA: Haven't you learned anything? There isn't more to it than that. We. Are. Nothing.

JAY: They shut us down completely. Like they already knew what their answer was gonna be.

VANESSA: They let us do all this work for nothing. They must be having a good laugh at our expense right now.

SIMONE: We'll just have to find another way.

VANESSA: What other way, wannabe?!

SIMONE: Why are you mad at me?

VANESSA: When did this become important to you, anyway? Last week? Last month? I've been working on this for a long time. Being Black didn't become important to me just because I'm crushing on a boy. So spare me your sympathies. You can go back and play pretend soul woman with your little dance duo. I was Black yesterday, I'm Black today, and I'll be Black tomorrow.

JAY: *(to VANESSA)* Don't be so hard on her.

VANESSA: Bro, please. You know that straight up it's not the same for her and me.

VANESSA holds her arm up next to SIMONE's.

Look at this closely. You get it? How many times have you been followed in a store when you shop with your White friends? How many times have the cops stopped to frisk you when you're with your White friends?

JAY: Vanessa!!

VANESSA: What, Jay? You don't want her to know what happened to you?

(to SIMONE) Jay and his brother were stopped by the police because they were wearing hoodies. They were looking for someone who robbed a dep and they stopped and frisked Jay!

SIMONE: What?

JAY: Vanessa . . . Shut. Up.

VANESSA: *(to JAY)* Don't Vanessa me. Why are you afraid to tell her what it really means to be Black? Are you scared she'll change her mind and hide back in her Whiteness?

SIMONE: Wait a minute. I know something about being Black—

VANESSA: *(to SIMONE)* Do you? Do you know how many times this school has threatened to suspend me because I can't take another teacher disrespecting me while every other student who isn't Black gets handled with kid gloves. Yo, Jay, tell her. They hate us. And we have to be all nice and calm, like her. Naw, man. Girl, you take your light skin privilege on out of here. You take your obedience and patience and understanding and take it somewhere else. Cuz right now, right this minute, right here, I just want to scream. Because this isn't fair. This isn't just. And I am so fed up of trying and trying. I'm so done with all this bullshit.

> *VANESSA stomps off.*

SIMONE: Vanessa, wait!

(to JAY) Why is she always so angry?

> *JAY winces.*

I can't believe the police stopped you. It doesn't make any sense.

> *Beat.*

Are you okay?

JAY: I don't want to talk about it.

SIMONE: Why didn't you tell me what happened to you?

JAY shakes his head.

You should've told me.

JAY ignores her and leaves.

Jay!

SIMONE is left standing alone.

Scene 15

SIMONE carries the laptop and projector following the spat with JAY and VANESSA.

SARAH: Hey! Simone! Wait up!

SIMONE stops.

We made it! We made it! We're in the talent show!

SIMONE: *(on the verge of tears)* Congratulations.

SARAH: I'm sorry I got so mad the other day. You were right. The judges didn't notice your mistake.

Beat.

What's the matter? Why aren't you happy? We made it!

SIMONE: Our proposal for Black History and Culture is dead.

SARAH: What do you mean dead?

SIMONE: Our proposal was rejected by the principal.

SARAH: Oh, that's too bad. But that means you can focus on the talent show!!

SIMONE shakes her head.

Hey, look, February isn't far away. Black History Month is just around the corner.

SIMONE: Black History Month is supposed to make me feel better? We get one month. Out of twelve. That's all the time you have for my culture and friends.

SARAH: One month is a lot.

SIMONE: You couldn't even come to jump up with me.

SARAH: Oh my Gawwwwwd, Simone. That was in the summer. Get over it. We have all Christmas break to perfect our routine. Maybe we can come up with even better costumes.

SIMONE: Are you even listening to yourself?

SARAH: What?

SIMONE just stares blankly at her.

Hey, I didn't kill your project—

SIMONE: You don't care one bit about my project.

SARAH: You told me White people weren't allowed so—

SIMONE: You're mad because of that?

SARAH: You're the one who's mad. Me, I just want to dance—

SIMONE: But you don't want to listen. Your dad called me mulatto but you don't care. Your brother posts MAGA memes on his Insta but you don't care.

SARAH: They don't mean anything by it!

SIMONE: You're constantly reminding me that I'm not Black. And that time that Eric yelled out in the caf, "BHCC—Black Hysterical Crybaby Community!!" You laughed along with everyone else.

SARAH: You shouldn't let stuff like that get to you . . .

SIMONE: I just wanted to work on this one project to learn more about where I come from, about my roots, but you had to turn it into a problem in your special little world.

SARAH: But the talent show is a fundraiser. You said that. If you're so Black, why don't you care about the poor little African kids!!!

SIMONE glares at her one last time, then leaves. SARAH is startled with realization.

I'm sorry! I meant the Malawians!

It's too late. SIMONE is gone.

Scene 16

SIMONE is alone in her room with her journal open.

ADULT AND CHILDREN'S VOICES: Half and half. Half-breed. Half-caste. Half-blood. Coloured. Quadroon. Octoroon. Mixed-race. Mixed-up. Messed-up. Mulatto.

SIMONE: We used to spend Christmas up north with my mom's family when I was a kid. I had this one *cousin* who was way older than me—he was my favourite. He'd have the best playlist with Rihanna and Bruno Mars, and we'd try out dance moves. I adored him. That's why my mom and I were so excited when he came over the other day, out of the blue. He got married a few months ago and wanted to share his wedding video with us. So we sat down in the living room with him to watch it. My dad was out at the time. So we get to this part where it showed everyone arriving at the wedding reception, at a hall in Saint-Eustache, on some country road. The sound was on, and you could hear the videographer and a buddy of his talking a bit. So we're watching all these White people arrive at the reception; you know, "pure laine." And then my family arrives, my mom, my dad, and me. "Oh! There you are!" my cousin says. Yeah! That's us. Cool! I mean, at this point I'm just really excited because my cousin is visiting my house and that makes me happy. And he's happy about getting married. We're all happy. Then I hear the videographer on the DVD say, "R'garde! C'est le nègre!" And for a millisecond, I'm like "What the—!" And I glance over at my mom and she's still smiling. But there's a weird look in her eyes. I know she's wondering if I heard it too. But we keep watching the video; my cousin is so happy about his wedding, I don't know if he's choosing to ignore it or just didn't hear it or just doesn't care . . . So, yah, in that moment, I wasn't excited or happy anymore that my cousin came over . . . But we kept smiling the rest of the time as if it never happened. And we never spoke about it afterward. Ever.

Change of lighting.

Scene 17

SIMONE sits alone at school writing in her journal.

SARAH approaches her, but SIMONE remains indifferent.

SARAH: *(trying to peek over SIMONE's shoulder)* What are you working on? Is that a poem?

SIMONE: *(embarrassed, folding her journal shut)* What do you want?

SARAH: I just wanted to know what you're working on!

SIMONE stares at SARAH.

You know, I need help with math.

SIMONE: You always need help with math.

SARAH: Well, since you're not talking to me, I'm going to fail, and I'll never go to university.

SIMONE: Right.

> *SARAH stays put.*

Okay, what are you having trouble with?

> *SARAH eagerly joins SIMONE at the table. She starts to take some books out of her backpack, none of which are math related. She stops.*

SARAH: You know . . .

> *SIMONE sighs and goes back to her journal.*

Simone, I'm so sorry.

SIMONE: About . . . ?

SARAH: I haven't been very good at listening.

> *Beat.*

For a long time.

> *Beat.*

I spent Christmas really listening to my family talking, and you're right. They're so bad.

Beat.

You know. "Immigrants are ruining our country." "Black people are criminals, so when they get shot it's because they did something wrong." I got so mad I left the dinner table.

SIMONE: You didn't.

SARAH: I sure did. But my dad got really mad at me, so I had to go back to the table. But I had earplugs in.

SIMONE: No way.

SARAH: I did, and I'll keep doing it.

Beat.

Listen, Simone, I haven't been a great friend . . .

Beat.

I'm so basic.

Beat.

I'm not sure what to do to make things better . . .

SIMONE: Me neither . . .

SARAH: I'm sorry your project was rejected.

SIMONE: Jay and I aren't even talking...

SARAH: What? I thought the two of you were—

SIMONE: We're not.

SARAH: Oh, wow...

> *Beat.*

I'm trying to come up with a solo piece for the show. All I have is March break to get ready, you know.

SIMONE: I'm sure you'll be fine.

SARAH: It won't be the same without you...

> *The school bell rings.*

Scene 18

> *SIMONE walks alone in the school hallway when she suddenly comes face to face with JAY.*

SIMONE: Hey.

JAY: Hey.

There's a moment of uncertainty. JAY is about to leave.

SIMONE: This has to stop.

JAY stays motionless.

We need to talk instead of avoiding each other.

JAY: You're going to make me talk about something I don't want to talk about.

SIMONE: You went through something horrible. We can't pretend it didn't happen.

JAY: I'm fine with it.

SIMONE: You don't look it.

Beat.

I thought we were friends or— How could you not share what happened with me?

JAY: That's why you're mad at me?

SIMONE: Vanessa seemed to know what happened, but you never told me anything.

JAY: My brother told her brother who told her. I never told Vanessa anything.

SIMONE: Oh . . .

JAY: Like . . . there's nothing to tell . . .

SIMONE: You were racially profiled. That's not okay.

JAY: Talking about it isn't gonna change anything.

SIMONE: I just want to know that you're all right. That they didn't hurt you.

JAY: You know what? I'm not okay. I've never hurt anyone or committed a crime in my whole life, but the cops saw fit to stop and frisk me anyway. I was humiliated . . . in front of a crowd in the middle of the Metro station . . . They had their guns held out, and I was so scared. I was shaking like a leaf for hours after it happened . . . and . . . and . . . I cried, Simone. I'm a wimp. And I didn't want you to know the truth. I'm ashamed that I was so afraid. That I couldn't be braver, like all those heroes we read about. We're fighting for the cause but I'm a . . . I'm a coward . . .

SIMONE: You are not a coward. Don't ever say that about yourself. You walk every day in this world with brown skin. You're a warrior.

JAY: You really think that?

SIMONE: Yes.

Shyness from both.

We can't give up on the BHCC. I feel like there's more that can be done.

JAY: What's the point when the principal won't listen?

SIMONE: We have to make her listen.

JAY: Simone, just let it go.

SIMONE: Are you doing anything?

JAY: Right now?

SIMONE: Yah?

JAY: I was just going home.

SIMONE: No! You're coming with me!

JAY: What?!

SIMONE grabs him by the hand.

SIMONE: Come on!

JAY follows, incredulous and laughing.

Scene 19

SIMONE and JAY enter her bedroom. She heads for a pile of papers in a folder similar to the ones VANESSA had pulled out at the second BHCC meeting.

SIMONE: Leave the door open. Or my mom'll get mad.

JAY shrugs.

(showing him the papers) Look, I found these in the material Vanessa gave us. It's about these religions in the Caribbean and Brazil that are a blend of West African beliefs and European Christianity—

JAY: They're mixed.

SIMONE: What?

JAY: Half and half, like you.

SIMONE: Right! So these beliefs survived the crossing of the Atlantic and slavery, and four hundred years later, they still exist: Shango, Obeah, Candomblé, Santeria, Vodou. You see, I keep wondering why everyone says my great-great-grandmother didn't say anything, but she was just trying to survive like everyone else, through having their drums and religions and dancing and cultures banned. If you look back, what our ancestors had to face is so much more difficult than what we have to face now. They had it so much harder than we do. But they still fought through it. They resisted. Like with Vodou and Obeah. And steel pan. And African rhythms. But we have it so much easier . . .

She looks intently at JAY.

That's why we can't give up, Jay. We owe it to them. We have to keep going no matter what the principal says. Look:

She opens a page of her journal.

" . . . Yemaya, who rules the oceans, is the mother of all the orishas and the protector of her children . . . "

JAY smiles but doesn't say anything.

What?

JAY: The student has become the teacher.

> *They laugh. She sits on the bed next to JAY. This might be a good
> time for them to kiss for the first time.*

MOM: *(voice-over)* Simone!!!!!

> *They put space between themselves.*
>
> *Blackout.*

Scene 20

> *Lights suddenly back up. In the school cafeteria, SARAH and
> VANESSA are sitting in different sections.*
>
> *JAY and SIMONE arrive carrying placards. SIMONE waves at
> SARAH, but they head to VANESSA.*
>
> *VANESSA grimaces as she sees them.*

VANESSA: No.

SIMONE: You didn't answer our texts.

VANESSA: I'm not getting involved. If you want to protest, that's
your business. I'm not getting suspended again.

JAY: Suspended? Who cares! That's like a vacation!

VANESSA: Fool. In my house it's no cell, no movies, no going out.

SIMONE: You started the BHCC. You did all this work. We can't do this without you.

JAY: You could do with some time off your phone.

VANESSA: Boiiii.

SIMONE: Vanessa, this is serious.

VANESSA doesn't answer.

(to JAY) Okay. . . it's just going to be you and me.

VANESSA shakes her head.

JAY and SIMONE head to the principal's office and plant themselves there.

They pull out signs that placed together read "Black History Matters."

The school bell rings but they don't budge.

SARAH's curious about what's going on and walks over to VANESSA.

SARAH: What are they doing?

VANESSA: It's a sit-in.

SARAH: What's a sit-in?

VANESSA gives SARAH side-eye and decides to join SIMONE and JAY.

JAY: Queen.

JAY gives her one of the signs to hold up.

SIMONE: I'm so glad you're here!

VANESSA: Yah, let's see how long it takes before they squash this.

They keep holding up the signs.

There is a stretched-out moment of inactivity.

Nothing happens.

Meanwhile, SARAH lurks around, like a kid wanting to join the other kids on the playground but is too scared to ask.

Okay, nothing's happening.

They drop their signs.

SIMONE: This isn't what I was expecting.

VANESSA: They don't seem to be bothered that we're here . . . We need to make it harder for them. Nobody in this school cares about this.

SIMONE: Not the Black students . . . Not the White students . . .

JAY: *(to SIMONE)* That poem you wrote about Yemaya.

SIMONE: What about it?

JAY: Let's recite it.

SIMONE: Uh . . . Why?

JAY: Uh, it's awesome.

> *SARAH, who's been eavesdropping the whole time, makes a decision and approaches the group.*

SARAH: Hey! I have an idea! What if you go live on Insta to get the word out to people? Vanessa, can I borrow your phone?

VANESSA: That's a pretty good idea!

> *VANESSA hands over her phone. SARAH goes live.*

SARAH: *(doing the TV host job she's always dreamed of)* We're here at the principal's office for the Black History and Culture Committee sit-in.

> *VANESSA, SIMONE, and JAY stand up one by one as they begin to recite a poem SIMONE wrote.*

SIMONE: I rise, like the wave at the tide, to rip from your mind old ideas that were lies.

VANESSA: I rise like the storm in the morn to restore your mind from brainwash to thought.

JAY: I rise like a tsunami of truth to put in reverse the whitewash in you.

VANESSA, JAY, & SIMONE: We rise, Yemaya as the sea, cleansing and rebirth, cured of amnesia.

VANESSA: Remember me, I rise.

JAY: Remember me, I rise.

SIMONE: Remember me, I rise.

VANESSA, JAY, & SIMONE: Builders of kingdoms, poets and authors, composers and healers, and people of science.

VANESSA: Do you want to go to the moon?

VANESSA, JAY, & SIMONE: Freedom fighters, nation builders.

JAY: Yes, this very nation.

VANESSA, JAY, & SIMONE: We rise as the wave, as Yemaya. We invite you to bathe in the ocean of memory, of knowledge. How can you deny us?

For if we, you and I, know not whence we came, we cannot know to where we, you and I, are heading.

There are a few hand claps, surprising all four.

SARAH turns the cellphone outward.

SARAH: Cool! Some students came down from class!

VANESSA: Better late than never!!

PRINCIPAL: *(voice-over)* Attention, students. You must return to your classes immediately or else you will be sent to detention.

A few students jeer.

SARAH: *(to VANESSA)* What should we do?

VANESSA: *(to SARAH)* Keep filming!

SIMONE: *(directly into the camera)* Come down. Come all.

VANESSA, SIMONE, and JAY form a huddle.

VANESSA: Follow my lead.

She turns back to face SARAH, who keeps filming and posting on social media.

We're here. We're Black. We're never going back.

SIMONE joins in now, adding some step-dance moves.

VANESSA & SIMONE: We're here. We're Black. We're never going back.

JAY and VANESSA pick up the step moves as JAY joins in on the chant.

VANESSA, JAY, & SIMONE: We're here. We're Black. We're never going back.

As they repeat the chant and the steps, new student voices are added as they join the sit in.

SARAH pans to capture all the new people joining the protest.

The cheer gets louder, becoming thunderous by the end as even more students have assembled.

VANESSA, JAY, SIMONE, & VOICES: We're here. We're Black. We're never going back. We're here. We're Black. We're never going back. We're here. We're Black. We're never going back.

PRINCIPAL: *(voice-over)* Vanessa Johnson, please report to the principal's office immediately. I repeat. Vanessa Johnson, report to the principal's office immediately.

Everyone looks at VANESSA, alarmed.

VANESSA: Okay, this is it. I'm gonna go see what she has to say. If I don't come back . . .

JAY: We'll send out a search party.

VANESSA puts on a brave face and leaves. Meanwhile, SIMONE and JAY pace nervously, awaiting her return.

SIMONE: Do you think they're gonna suspend her?

JAY: I don't know . . . Let's wait and see . . .

SARAH hovers around, filming with the cellphone. SIMONE shoos her away like a fly.

SARAH moves on to JAY, who does the same.

SIMONE: What do you think's happening?

JAY: I don't know . . .

VANESSA finally returns. All eyes are on her.

SIMONE, JAY, & SARAH: What happened? What did she say?

VANESSA takes a deep breath.

VANESSA: *(to all the students)* They want to set up a meeting to discuss this further.

JAY, SIMONE, & SARAH: What?!

VANESSA: They want to meet with us in a week to go over our proposal. They're going to give us a chance.

(to everyone) We did it!!! We did it!!! They're gonna listen to us!

A huge cheer breaks out from all the students, as if the school basketball team had just scored the winning basket.

SARAH watches, thrilled, as VANESSA, SIMONE, and JAY dance and whoop it up.

They jump and laugh. SARAH *joins in. All four of them end up in a group hug.*

VANESSA *pulls away, realizing she's too cool for group hugs.* SARAH *pulls away, realizing she's not Black.*

SIMONE *and* JAY *are hugging and all of a sudden it's awkward. They draw apart, shy and embarrassed.*

We've moved a step closer to achieving our goal today.

SIMONE: Congratulations!!

VANESSA: Thank you for bringing us back together.

JAY: The poem was a nice touch. "We rise . . . !"

SIMONE: Thanks.

JAY: I messed up. I shoulda told you about the cops.

SARAH: I did too. I shoulda listened more.

VANESSA *becomes annoyed with all the emotion.*

VANESSA: We all screwed up! Enough with the guilt trips. Listen, we still have a lot of work to do. We need to start getting ready for next week's meeting.

VANESSA *leaves with a sense of urgency to pursue her mission.*

SARAH: She's . . . like . . . our very own . . . Michelle Obama.

SARAH, in awe, is about to follow VANESSA.

SIMONE: Sarah! Let's meet later to talk about the talent show. I have some ideas I want us to look at.

SARAH: What? Are you serious? Thank you, Simone. I love you so much. I still have our costumes in my locker. I'll go get them.

SARAH disappears in a flash, leaving SIMONE and JAY chuckling.

Beat.

JAY: You joining the committee was the best thing that happened to me all year.

SIMONE: You telling me about the committee was the best thing that happened to me all year.

Their hands brush together as the lights go out.

Scene 21

All silent.

SIMONE is in her room again, alone.

SIMONE: I keep thinking of Soledad Rouseau, who sitting, rocking, rocking, rocking in her chair, was so quiet. What did she see? Her grandchildren all shades of brown. Diluted. Different. Distant from her past and what she had once known. What was jump up again? A link to the past. Our past. The anchor. The roots. The grounding.

A parade of people celebrating the past, churning forward. You kept quiet, Soledad, but I can speak for you now. And for me. I know who I am, and no one can take that away.

All of a sudden:

JAY: Eh, eh, Simone! Let's play mas!!

Soca music blares.

SARAH, JAY, and VANESSA are wearing their carnival costumes. As they dance, they adorn SIMONE with her costume and start "jumping" at Carifiesta on René Lévesque Boulevard in downtown Montreal.

SARAH and SIMONE give a little snippet of what their talent show routine was, with JAY and VANESSA trying to pick up the moves . . .

The end.

Bibliography

"16 Inspiring Quotes from the Civil Rights Movement." *MSN*, 1 Feb. 2016, http://www.msn.com/en-us/news/us/16-inspiring-quotes-from -the-civilrights-movement/ss-AA8VYSr#image=16.

"African Poems: Oral Poetry from Africa." http://www.africanpoems.net/.

Barbeau, Julie. Interview. Jun. 2016.

Bingham, Russell. "Viola Desmond." *Historica Canada*, 27 Jan. 2013, http://www.thecanadianencyclopedia.ca/en/article/viola -desmond/.

Cooper, Afua. "Marie-Joseph Angélique." *Historica Canada*, 18 Feb. 2014, http://www.thecanadianencyclopedia.ca/en/article /marie-joseph-angelique/.

Hird, Ed. "Governor James Douglas: Father of BC." *Edhird's Blog*, 22 Jul. 2010, https://edhird.com/2010/07/22/governor-james-douglas -father-of-bc/.

Hoffman, Cindy. Interview. Jun. 2016.

Inger, Mariah. Interview. Jun. 2016.

Lasher, Megan. "Read The Full Transcript Of Jesse Williams' Powerful Speech On Race At The BET Awards." *Time* , 27 Jun. 2016, http://time.com/4383516/jesse-williams-bet-speech-transcript/.

Latour, Enrico. Interview. Jun. 2016.

Mahtani, Minelle. *Mixed Race Amnesia: Resisting the Romanticization of Multiculturality*. UBC Press, 2014.

Paul, Christian Frederic. Interview. Jun. 2016.

Sangweni, Yolanda. "The Way-Too-Short List of Black Oscar Winners." *Essence*, 30 Mar. 2019, https://www.essence.com/celebrity /way-too-short-list-black-oscar-winners/#342911.

Sedgwick, Marcus. "From Thor to Odin: A guide to the Norse gods." *The Guardian*, 4 Feb. 2015, https://www.theguardian.com /world/2015/feb/04/thor-odin-norse-gods-guide-iceland-temple -vikings-deities.

"Trinidad Carnival: The Birth & Evolution." *Discover Trinidad & Tobago*, 24 Feb. 2022, https://www.discovertnt.com/articles/Trinidad/ The-Birth-Evolution-of-Trinidad-Carnival/109/3 /32#axzz4SIS7GW2u.

"We Talk to Interracial Couples 50 Years After Loving vs. Virginia." Vice News, *YouTube*, uploaded by VICE News, 13 Jun. 2017, https://www.youtube.com/watch?v=RseBL4eCook.

Williams, Dr. Eric. *History of the People of Trinidad and Tobago*. PNM Publishing, 1962.

Acknowledgements

I wish to acknowledge that while *Simone, Half and Half* tells the tale of displaced African people with lost languages, cultures, and beliefs, this story takes place on the traditional territory of the Kanien'kehá:ka people, who also share similar experiences. The land was a diplomatic meeting place with other Iroquoians and Algonquians, including Algonquin-Anishinaabe, Atikamekw, and Huron-Wendat. I recognize that I am located on a land that has been the site of human creativity and storytelling for thousands of years, and I'm thankful that I am able to live, create, collaborate, and work here. Niá:wen.

Christine Rodriguez is the award-winning playwright of *Dreaming in Autism*, which earned third prize at Ottawa Little Theatre's 72nd National One-Act Playwriting Competition. *Simone, Half and Half*, commissioned and produced in 2020 by Black Theatre Workshop, received five Montreal English Theatre Award nominations, including one for Outstanding New Text. Christine's first short film, *Fuego*, an Official Selection of the 2021 American Black Film Festival, was written and filmed in English, French, and Spanish. Thanks to *Fuego*, she was nominated for Filmmaker of the Year by Gala Dynastie, which recognizes Black excellence in Québec. Following stints with the Warner Bros. Discovery Access x Canadian Academy Writers Program and the Rogers/Black Screen Office Development Fund in 2021, Christine took part in the Norman Jewison Film Program Writers' Lab at the Canadian Film Centre from July to December 2022. She holds an M.B.A. from McGill University and a Certificate of Professional Screenwriting from UCLA. She's currently working on obtaining a major in Hispanic Studies from Université de Montréal. Christine's work is largely informed by her mixed-race Afro-Trinidadian heritage and her multicultural environment. She lives in Montréal.